A Canadian Museum of Nature Book

Sea Monsters

Written By
Stephen Cumbaa

Illustrated By
Margot Thompson

Kids Can Press

I blame my Dad, Bill Cumbaa, for my fascination with creatures of the lakes and seas. All those fishing trips, our stories about "the big one that got away," and adventures with alligators left their mark. This one's for you, Dad. — S.C.

Acknowledgments

My colleagues Tamaki Sato and Xiao-chun Wu generously shared with me their time and expertise on very real ancient sea monsters — giant fossil crocodiles, mosasaurs and plesiosaurs. Ed Bousfield helped by sharing his research and his enthusiasm for Cadborosaurus.

Thanks to Margot Thompson for so artfully breathing life into the monsters on these pages, and to Julia Naimska for the great design. Many thanks go to my editor, Liz MacLeod, for keeping this project on track. Her clever suggestions, sense of humor, attention to detail and cheery pep talks were much appreciated.

Finally, special thanks to Bruce Williams for his unwavering support, and to my family for giving of their time with me to make this book possible.

Kids Can Press acknowledges the financial support of the Government of Ontario, through the Ontario Media Development Corporation's Ontario Book Initiative; the Ontario Arts Council; the Canada Council for the Arts; and the Government of Canada, through the BPIDP, for our publishing activity.

Published in Canada by
Kids Can Press Ltd.
29 Birch Avenue
Toronto, ON M4V 1E2

Published in the U.S. by
Kids Can Press Ltd.
2250 Military Road
Tonawanda, NY 14150

www.kidscanpress.com

The artwork in this book was rendered in oil.
The text is set in Meridien.

Edited by Elizabeth MacLeod
Designed by Julia Naimska
Printed and bound in Singapore

The hardcover edition of this book is smyth sewn casebound.
The paperback edition of this book is limp sewn with a drawn-on cover.

CM 07 0 9 8 7 6 5 4 3 2 1
CM PA 07 0 9 8 7 6 5 4 3 2 1

Library and Archives Canada Cataloguing in Publication

Cumbaa, Stephen L.
   Sea monsters / written by Stephen Cumbaa ; illustrated by Margot Thompson.

Includes index.
ISBN-13: 978-1-55337-559-3 (bound)
ISBN-10: 1-55337-559-9 (bound)
ISBN-13: 978-1-55337-560-9 (pbk.)
ISBN-10: 1-55337-560-2 (pbk.)

1. Marine animals — Juvenile literature. 2. Sea monsters — Juvenile literature. I. Title.

QL122.2.C86 2007   j591.77   C2006-903627-6

Kids Can Press is a *l'* ©𝗿𝗎𝘀™ Entertainment company

Photo Credits
Every reasonable effort has been made to trace ownership of, and give accurate credit to, copyrighted material. Information that would enable the publisher to correct any discrepancies in future editions would be appreciated.

p. 22: American Museum of Natural History/ Bashford Dean; **p. 31:** Vo Trung Dung/Corbis/Sygma/ Magma; **p. 32:** Sandra Mansi; **p. 36:** British Columbia Archives and Record Service/I-61404; **p. 38:** Courtesy U.S. Navy Visual News.

CONTENTS

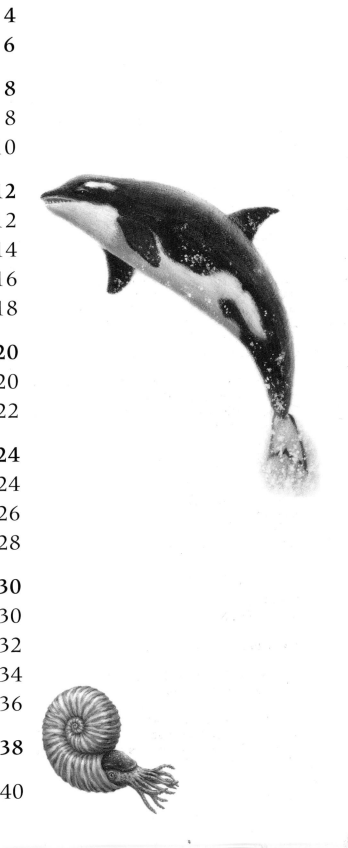

Sea Monsters?

It was late one night, far out in the middle of the ocean. Suddenly, the dark water began to bubble and foam. Something rose high above the surface. A gigantic tentacle shot out of the darkness and thumped the deck! Then the monstrous arm slid back into the murky depths. Not one of the terrified crew slept that night.

Those sailors called the beast a sea monster and told their chilling story to others. It was easy to believe such tales. Long ago, before people knew much about the world, explorers sailed off to find unknown lands. They had heard lots of myths and legends. They expected to find strange people and unknown creatures.

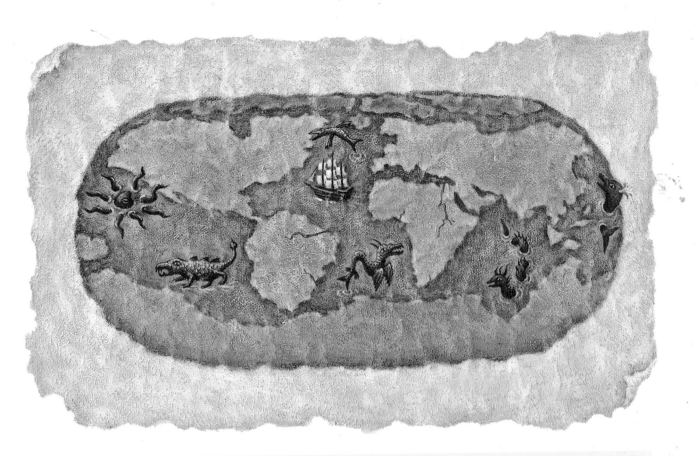

Some ancient maps have a label at the edge of unexplored oceans that says, "There be monsters!" Sometimes this was a real warning. But other times it was to scare people away from interesting places!

Today, most of the world has been explored, and people know a lot more about science. But it turns out that some of those stories about sea monsters attacking ships are true. And people are still seeing strange, giant beasts in the ocean or in lakes and rivers.

Deep waters are dark and mysterious places. Enormous animals, some that almost no one has ever seen, may live in the depths. Scientists are exploring far below the ocean's surface to discover if any of these creatures are real.

Fossil bones of real sea monsters have been found around the world. Most of these huge beasts were dead before any people were around to be frightened of them. Some of these ancient animals were really scary and very dangerous.

So which sea monsters are extinct? Did some actually exist? Which creatures live in the ocean, and which live only in the imagination? Join the hunt as scientists try to decide.

It's Tough Being a Monster!

Imagine how difficult it would be to find a place to live if you were a sea monster. If you were really huge, you would need lots of room. Deep lakes and wide oceans would be best. Those give you space to swim, to explore — and even to hide.

All that room is nice, but deep water is always dark, and almost always cold. You would have to have great big eyes to see. To stay warm, you would have to keep moving.

If you were a sea monster, you would also need lots of animals to hunt. Being big means having to catch and eat a lot of food. You would eat mostly slithery or scaly creatures, unless you count a few ships.

Everyone would be scared of you if you were a sea monster. Most people would race away from you as fast as they could. Some would try to kill you. Others would like to take your picture, or capture or study you. If you did get caught, you would become famous.

Large animals such as sea monsters eat so much that each one needs an enormous hunting area. That means probably living a long way from other sea monsters. It could be hard to find a mate and have a family.

But being a sea monster just might be worth it. Imagine the fun you would have bumping into a boat, or zipping past and scaring everyone in it.

LEGENDS COME ALIVE

People have told stories about sea monsters for hundreds of years. Then something really scary happened — some of the tales turned out to be true!

Kraken

One October evening in 1873 near Portugal Cove, Newfoundland, a huge creature attacked some fishermen. Many long, powerful arms snaked around their rowboat and began to crush it. The terrified men escaped by hacking off two of the arms with a hatchet. They saved the largest arm, which was almost twice the length of their boat.

People now think that this giant sea monster fits the description of a legendary creature. In Scandinavia, they called this ancient beast the kraken. Most scientists had thought stories of this monster were just tall tales. When they saw the severed arm, they knew it was a real animal: a giant squid.

What an amazing creature! By changing the color of its skin, the giant squid can seem to disappear. Or it can squirt out a cloud of ink to hide. By sucking in water, then squirting it, this sea monster can race through the water.

The giant squid has huge, strong muscles in its eight arms and two longer tentacles. The bottom sides of all ten are covered with cup-like suckers. They help this beast hold on tight to its dinner.

The edges of the suckers in one kind of giant squid have enormous, razor-sharp hooks. They help this hunter get a death grip on its victims. A squid's mouth has a big, parrot-like beak that easily cuts and tears flesh.

Giant squid can be longer than a basketball court is wide. They have eyes the size of dinner plates — the largest of any living animal. Those huge eyes help giant squid hunt at night in deep, dark water.

Devilfish

Sailors used to tell stories of giant, eight-armed monsters they called devilfish. They said these creatures were evil, bloodthirsty and strong enough to sink ships. Drawings and descriptions of the monstrous devilfish seem to fit huge octopuses.

More than 100 years ago, a giant blob washed up near St. Augustine, Florida.

The shark-bitten lump weighed as much as an elephant. Some scientists identified it as the head of a huge octopus. The outstretched arms of an octopus this big would almost touch the hoops at each end of a basketball court!

The biggest type of octopus that scientists are sure really exists is the giant octopus of the Pacific Ocean. The largest one known had arms as long as two large canoes. This sea creature was caught off the coast of British Columbia, Canada.

Octopuses are great hunters. They move quickly. They change color to become almost invisible on the ocean bottom. Octopuses are also very smart. They can easily figure out how to slip through small openings to catch their dinner.

Each of an octopus's eight arms has two rows of suckers, which give it a great grip. And these beasts are incredibly strong. A medium-sized octopus can lift three adults. How strong could an octopus be that is 10 to 15 times larger?

Fishermen in the Bahama Islands swear that monster octopuses live deep in the ocean. That may be true, but who would volunteer to dive down to find such a big, smart, dangerous sea monster?

ANCIENT MONSTERS

Long ago, when dinosaurs ruled the land, giant sea monsters were the terror of the ocean. These ancient creatures, like the dinosaurs, were real. Scientists know this because they have found sea monster fossils.

Old Big Eyes

Some of the largest sea monsters were the fish-lizards, or ichthyosaurs (ICK-thee-oh-sawrz). These hunters were fast, powerful swimmers and deep divers. They could chase their prey as far below the ocean's surface as the length of six football fields.

Scientists think ichthyosaurs hunted fish, squid and turtles at night. Their huge eyes and good vision made it easy for them to chase their dinner in the dark. That's when many creatures of the sea come out of hiding. Lots of sharp teeth in their narrow jaws kept dinner from slipping away.

The fossil skeleton of a truly monstrous ichthyosaur was discovered in British Columbia, Canada, in 1992. This beast was as long as two big school buses. It probably weighed more than 1000 fourth graders!

The head of this ancient sea monster was as big as a minivan. Its jaws were longer than a tall adult. When this ichthyosaur was alive 220 million years ago, it was the most enormous animal on Earth.

An ichthyosaur's eyes were huge — larger than dinner plates.

Necks and Jaws

Plesiosaurs (PLEEZ-ee-oh-sawrz) once lived in all the world's oceans. Animals they chased did not stand a chance. A plesiosaur could almost "fly" through water. It used its flippers as if they were wings, and could change direction quickly.

Special bones in a plesiosaur's skeleton protected it from other hunters. In most animals, the belly is an easy place to attack. Not in a plesiosaur! Big, flat bones and ribs across its belly covered it on the inside like a suit of armor.

There were short-necked and long-necked plesiosaurs. The ones with short necks were called pliosaurs (PLY-oh-sawrz). They had huge heads. The largest of these monsters was almost as long as two classrooms. It had a skull the length of a small car and enormous curved, pointed teeth.

The jaws of this ferocious monster were bigger and stronger than the jaws of *Tyrannosaurus rex*. This beast ate sharks, ichthyosaurs (see page 12) and even other plesiosaurs. Nothing was safe when it was hungry.

Imagine a huge mouth full of big, sharp teeth. Now picture that mouth on the end of a neck about the length of your school classroom! This long-necked monster was a kind of plesiosaur called an elasmosaur (uh-LAS-mo-sawr).

These beasts had up to 70 neck bones — humans have only 7! That long, flexible neck could whip the elasmosaur's snapping jaws from side to side as it attacked fish.

Giant Sea Lizards

Picture giant, bloodthirsty lizards rocketing through the water. They gobble down anything in their path. Even sharks flee from them. These scary creatures from a nightmare were dangerous, and they were real. They were mosasaurs (MOE-zuh-sawrz).

Mosasaurs swam in all the oceans of the world while dinosaurs walked the land. They ate anything they could catch.

Scientists think mosasaurs could move from standing still to full speed in seconds. Maybe they hid in seaweed waiting to attack. The color

The largest mosasaur could just fit across an Olympic-sized swimming pool.

pattern of their scaly skin probably disguised them. It worked the same way as camouflage clothing worn by soldiers and hunters.

Unlike other sea monsters, mosasaurs probably hunted close to shore. They may have been able to swim up rivers from the sea. There these beasts could attack animals wading in shallow water. Mosasaurs could change direction quickly and easily. Few creatures escaped this hungry monster.

The long, pointed mouth of a mosasaur held thick, cone-shaped teeth. They easily crunched through shell or bone. The jaws had a hinge in the middle, similar to the one on a door. And the mosasaur's mouth would swing open wide so it could swallow an animal nearly as big as itself.

Helmet Heads

Dunkleosteus (duncle-OS-tea-us) lived 370 million years ago, long before the dinosaurs. Back then, it was the largest animal on Earth. It grew to be as long as a stretch limousine. Every living creature fled in terror from this huge hunter.

"Dunk's" skull was like a big helmet with a hinge in back. The hinge let this monster lift the top of the skull to open its jaws for a giant bite. Dunk could open its mouth wide enough to swallow an entire shark.

Dunk's razor-sharp jaws worked the same way jagged scissors do. They could easily chop anything in half.

Bony plates similar to armor surrounded the front part of Dunkleosteus's body.

"Helmet heads" came in all shapes and sizes. *Archelon* (AR-key-lon) was the largest turtle ever. *Archelon* may have lived to be more than 100 years old, so it had a lot of time to grow.

This sea monster was as big as a family swimming pool, and weighed as much as 25 men. *Archelon*'s mouth was a sharp, pointed beak, and its powerful jaws had sharp edges. It could open its mouth wide enough to chomp a large squid or swallow a big jellyfish.

Monster Chompers

Long ago, there were crocodiles and sharks much larger than any living today. These ancient sea monsters had enormous teeth and really knew how to use them.

Killer Crocs

Some of the scariest sea monsters living at the time of the dinosaurs were huge killer crocodiles. These crocs were so big they even hunted dinosaurs!

One giant croc from North America was *Deinosuchus* (dino-SUE-cuss). Its name means "terrible crocodile." "Deino" grew to be as long as the largest school bus, and weighed much more than a *Tyrannosaurus*. It had the strongest jaws of any animal ever. Deino could easily crush the shells of even enormous turtles.

Deino and other crocodiles were so huge they needed really big animals to eat. So they waited under the murky water. When a dinosaur plowed through the water looking for food, the croc lunged forward and chomped. Its strong teeth and jaws could snap even a dinosaur's leg bones with one bite.

Another "Super Croc" named *Sarcosuchus* (sar-ko-SUE-cuss) lived in Africa 110 million years ago. "Sarc" was about as big as Deino and was probably always just as hungry. This big snapper had more than 130 teeth in narrow jaws that were as long as a tall man.

Like all crocodiles, *Sarcosuchus* was protected by plates of bony armor under its skin. Its favorite snacks were huge fish and wading dinosaurs.

Megatooth Shark

Can you imagine a shark longer than the biggest city bus? Meet *Carcharocles megalodon* (car-CARE-oh-klees MEG-a-lo-don), one of the scariest sea monsters of all time.

"Meg" was the largest shark that ever lived. It was three times longer than *Tyrannosaurus* and five times heavier. An entire *T. rex* skull could easily fit inside the shark's jaws! This huge sea monster had even bigger teeth than that giant dinosaur.

This model of Meg's jaw is only slightly larger than the real thing. Those are real fossil teeth in the jaw! This sea monster's teeth have been found in warm oceans all over the world.

Meg's mouth could open so that it was taller than your front door. That meant there wasn't much this shark couldn't eat. Meg was also a superfast swimmer. It could catch almost anything it wanted for dinner.

The second word in Meg's name, "megalodon," means "great tooth." Meg had more than 200 teeth, each one as big as a man's hand. They were triangle shaped and arranged in about five rows. The edges of each tooth were similar to steak knives, with sharp, sawlike points.

This enormous shark could chomp down whales for lunch. How do scientists know that? They have found ancient whale bones sliced through by Meg's amazing teeth and powerful bite.

LIVING MONSTERS

Did you know that giant animals still live in our oceans and lakes? Most live so deep or so far from shore that they are rarely seen. These creatures are so strange that when people see one, they often say they have seen a sea monster.

Living Fossils

Scientists call the sturgeon a living fossil. That's because this fish has changed very little from the way its relatives looked millions of years ago. Today, sturgeons live in lakes, rivers and oceans, just as they did at the time of the dinosaurs.

The big, pointy plates along a sturgeon's back and sides are called scutes. They are made of bone and are hard enough to protect the fish the way armor does. The scutes make this sea monster look as if it is some kind of robot fish. A sturgeon also has tough skin that is as rough as sandpaper.

Sturgeons can live to be more than 100 years old and grow to be giants. The white sturgeon is the largest freshwater fish in North America. One caught in British Columbia in 1912 was as long as four Grade 5 kids lying down head to foot.

Usually sturgeons eat crayfish, insects and fish that they suck up from the bottom. But they can eat almost anything, even tin cans and small animals!

NOT-SO-GENTLE GIANTS

Whales are gentle giants most of the time. But when they are hunting or protecting their families, they can be dangerous.

To many animals of the sea, the orca, or killer whale, must be a really scary sea monster. Big orcas can be as long as school buses. They eat other whales, sharks, birds, walruses and even polar bears. With their strong teeth and jaws, they rip apart large animals.

Orcas are smart enough to work together in packs to hunt. From deep in the water, they watch seals and polar bears resting on big chunks of sea ice. One orca swims up under the ice and bumps it, so the seal slides off and into the mouth of the other orca.

Once an enormous sperm whale attacked a ship. The men on the boat were trying to harpoon the whale and his family. The whale blasted straight for the ship. He smashed his huge head through its side — twice — and sank it!

Sperm whales are as long as the distance from a baseball pitcher's mound to home plate. They can weigh as much as six or seven big African elephants. These huge whales have jaws as long as a minivan, full of teeth each the length of your foot.

There are no hunters on the planet today that are bigger than these blunt-headed whales. They hunt squid and fish in the deepest parts of the ocean. Large sharks may also find themselves on a sperm whale's menu.

Many sperm whales have big round scars on their skin. The marks are made by the suckers of giant squid.

Hunters and Flyers

It is hard to imagine an animal living today that is scarier than a shark. Sharks are fast and silent killers. They can smell the prey they are hunting from a distance as far away as four football fields. Their speed, power and huge appetite make them very dangerous.

A hungry shark will attack and eat almost anything. Fish, seals, dolphins and other water animals are normal food. Weird things found inside shark stomachs include a tire, a suit of armor and parts of people.

The great white is probably the shark most feared by people and sea creatures. It has even attacked boats. This supreme hunter can be as long as a school classroom. The sight of this monster's open mouth with all 230 teeth ready to chomp would terrify any creature. Even a touch of its rough hide brushing past can shred skin.

One of the strangest sea monsters of all is the manta ray, a close relative of sharks. Because of the hornlike fins on the manta's head, it was once called the giant devil ray. These giants fly through the water with their great wings. Each wing can stretch out as large as your living room.

This sea monster can be as heavy as an elephant. Mantas are also incredibly strong. They sometimes get caught in the anchor rope of a boat. When they race away, they may tow the boat with them.

Mantas often take off with a burst of speed and leap out of the water — as high as 5 m (16 ft.). They have been known to crush boats when they smack down on the water in belly flops.

Real or Not?

The most famous sea monsters of all may not be real. None have been captured. Photographs of them are blurry. But many scientists are still looking for these amazing creatures.

Loch Ness Monster

It is a foggy day for boating on Scotland's Loch Ness, but the big lake is calm. As you row toward shore, the water bubbles around the boat. Suddenly the lake rises under you! There is a stink in the air, but nothing to see except lots of bubbles and a few waves. Wait — was that something swimming away?

You may have just had a close encounter with the Loch Ness Monster. The first time "Nessie" was seen centuries ago, people claimed that it killed a man. As far as is known, the monster has not killed anyone since. A big reward was once offered for proof that Nessie is real, but no one was able to claim it.

Nessie is said to be about as long as four canoes, or maybe even a whale. A few years ago, scientists set up a special underwater camera in Loch Ness. It took some blurry photos of what might be a really huge animal. The pictures show shapes that seem to look like parts of a plesiosaur (see page 14).

Loch Ness is large and deep enough to hide a sea monster, but it became a lake only 10 000 years ago. That is millions of years after scientists think the last plesiosaur died.

Some think the strange things people see on the lake are waves caused by tiny earthquakes. Maybe the "monster" is bubbles of gas from leaves rotting on the lake's bottom. Or perhaps it really is the Loch Ness Monster, chasing fish such as salmon, sea trout or eels for dinner.

This photo of Nessie is now known to be a fake. But the dark waters of Loch Ness would be a great spot for a huge creature to hide.

Lake Monsters

Many people claim to have spotted lake monsters in Canada and the United States. Dozens, maybe hundreds, of sightings come from two very big lakes. Each seems to have its own giant beast.

"Champ" lives in Lake Champlain, between Quebec in Canada and New York and Vermont in the United States. It was first seen by explorers nearly 400 years ago. Before that, Native legends told of a lake monster like a large, horned snake.

Most sightings of Champ occur as night is falling. Perhaps that is when this lake creature surfaces to feed.

More than 70 people were out on Lake Champlain one night in July 1984. They were shocked to see what they thought were the coils of an enormous animal. The beast appeared to be as long as a bus.

The best evidence of the Lake Champlain Monster is this photo taken in 1977. The photographer's children were playing at the water's edge when the monster surfaced nearby and scared them!

Many people bring cameras to Lake Okanagan in British Columbia, hoping to snap a picture of "Ogopogo." Photos and videos in recent years show a huge, snaky creature in the lake.

Long before this beast became well known, Native people feared it. Their ancestors carved images of it on rocks. They named it *N'ha-a-itk*, or "Devil of the Lake." No hunter dared fish near an underwater cave where they thought it lived. Native people carried live animals in their canoes as gifts to the monster.

Nobody was able to claim the $2 million reward that was offered for proof that Ogopogo existed. But some scientists still think something big and strange lurks in Lake Okanagan.

Most reports of snakelike creatures are from long and very deep lakes, such as Lake Okanagan and Loch Ness. Is this the favorite kind of lake for monsters? Or is there something else about lakes this shape that fools lots of people? Scientists are still looking for answers.

Sea Serpent Tales

People claim to have seen sea monsters for more than 300 years along the coast of New England. Almost all of the stories describe a large snaky beast, called a sea serpent. It had a horselike head, which it often lifted above the waves. Some saw a spiky horn on its head.

A lot of people claimed they saw this amazing monster in August 1817. They said the huge sea serpent swam into the harbor of Gloucester, Massachusetts. Its body looked like a row of small barrels. Over the next few weeks, the beast, sometimes called the Gloucester Sea Serpent, was spotted almost every day.

Most people guessed the creature was as long as the largest whale. Some thought it moved

up and down in the water, the way a caterpillar scoots across a leaf. Everyone said the animal was a fast swimmer. Whalers and fishermen thought it had come into the harbor to hunt fish.

People tried to kill the sea serpent. One man shot it, but that only made the creature angry. The giant monster turned straight at him and dove under his boat. A whaling captain claimed he speared it with a huge harpoon. The beast raced off, towing the boat. Finally the harpoon tore free, and the sea serpent swam away.

In 1912, the crew of a fishing boat were pulling in a net full of fish when the Gloucester Sea Serpent attacked. With help from two other boats, they fought the creature for two hours until it died.

The men said they were too tired to tow the beast's body to shore, so there is no evidence of their struggle. No one has been able to explain what this sea serpent might have been.

Caddy

Sea monsters may prowl the waters of Cadboro Bay, near Victoria, British Columbia. They may have been lurking about for a long time. The Native people of the coast knew these creatures by many names. One is *Hiyitl'iik*, or "he who moves by wriggling from side to side."

Many recent sightings are of a beast that swims very quickly. As in the Native legends, some say it moves from side to side in the water. Others say this monster moves up and down, with coils like a Slinky toy. Most people see the head and neck first, sticking out of the water.

Some reports about *Cadborosaurus* or "Caddy" say this sea creature is larger than most fishing boats. It may even be as huge as a big whale.

In 1917, one man said he saw Caddy and shot at it. This animal has not attacked any people, but

Is this dead mystery creature a small *Cadborosaurus*? It was found in the stomach of a sperm whale in 1937.

it may once have snatched a duck away from two hunters. It has also been seen snapping at seagulls and chasing salmon and other fish. Some people have seen two monsters together, one large and one small.

Some people say Caddy hisses, others say it moos. This beast may even crawl up on land. A woman and her dog were terrified when they came upon this enormous, lizard-like creature on a beach. It quickly slithered into the water.

Despite these reports, few scientists think Caddy exists. Those that do think Caddy and Nessie (see page 30) could be plesiosaurs (see page 14). They think the size, the long neck and the body shape are almost the same.

No one has ever found the bones of any of these sea monsters. If a skeleton is found, scientists can compare it to plesiosaur bones to see if they match. If they do, we would know a lot more about these mysterious monsters.

NEW MONSTERS?

The oceans of the world are much larger than all of its land. In some places, the ocean is more than 11 km (7 mi.) deep. That's a lot of space to hide in, even if you are a huge monster.

Scientists are exploring this deep underwater world looking for creatures. What are the chances that they will find new sea monsters in the future? Will they finally capture one of the old beasts from stories and legends?

Hunting sea monsters is difficult, expensive and dangerous. It can also be fun and exciting. Exploration of the underwater world is possible with scuba gear and small submarines. New cameras, underwater radar and sound recording equipment help scientists learn more about the creatures of the sea.

There are still many mysteries about sea monsters. And scientists make new discoveries each year. In 2003, they found a new kind of giant squid. That same year, fossil bones of the world's largest plesiosaur were uncovered. Not long before that, Canadian scientists found the skeleton of the most enormous ichthyosaur ever.

Each of the scientists who has found a sea monster was once a kid. Will you be the one who someday makes the world's biggest sea monster discovery?

This rare oarfish is one of the world's longest fish. Could it be mistaken for a sea serpent?

Index